The Purim Story

The Purim Story

Rabbi Lance J. Sussman, Ph.D.

Published by Tablo

TABLE OF CONTENTS

"…sadness became happiness and mourning became joy"

Esther *9:22*

INTRODUCTION

"The Scroll of Esther" or *"Megillat Esther"* is one of the most beloved stories from the Hebrew Bible. Every year in the early spring, Jews around the world tell Esther's story during the holiday of Purim with great festivity, special foods, carnivals, the presentation of original Purim plays, singing, exchanging gifts and the giving of *Tzedakah* or charity. At the very heart of Purim is the reading or chanting of the Scroll of Esther.

In creating this new, illustrated "Scroll of Esther," our goal was to make the telling of the Purim Story accessible and fun for modern Jews, their families and anyone who simply wants to learn and enjoy this ancient tale. The original Hebrew text has been rendered into a modified narrative designed for reading aloud in English. The story itself has been streamlined and the number of complex Hebrew and Persian names has been reduced. Also, the frequency of the name **Haman**, the villain of the story who is booed in pubic readings of the Megillah, has been increased and presented in bold letters!

Marlene D'Orazio Adler, a Philadelphia based artist, has created a dozen original illustrations for this publication. To prepare herself for this project, Marlene visited a number of Judaic museums, examined numerous historic Megillot and studied ancient Persian art. Rita Rosen Poley, Director of the Temple Judea Museum of Reform Congregation Keneseth Israel, Elkins Park, Pennsylvania, carefully reviewed the narrative sections of this "Scroll of Esther." Chana R. Sussman oversaw the publication of *The Purim Story*.

We hope our *Purim Story* will become a regular part of your Purim celebrations. It can be read at home and at synagogue in preparation for or during the holiday. It can also be read at any time of year just for fun! We guarantee that it will be both fun and a learning experience

Have a Happy Purim and remember to boo the name of Haman!

CHAPTER 1: VASHTI

And it came to pass in the days of the King of Persia, Ahasuerus, who ruled from India to Ethiopia, 127 provinces, that the following story took place:

In the third year of his reign, Ahasuerus sat on his throne and made a huge feast which lasted 180 days. All the leading men of the kingdom attended. Lots of drinks were served, all in gold vessels. The Queen, Vashti, also made a feast for the women in the royal palace.

On the seventh day of the feast when the King was very drunk, he ordered Queen Vashti to come to his feast wearing only her royal crown but she refused and would not be humiliated. The King was furious.

Ahasuerus called his legal advisors and asked what to do about the Queen. They told him that not only was the Queen defying the King but that all the wives of husbands would become disobedient following her example. So, the King ordered that Vashti should no longer be the Queen. He then sent out a proclamation that all wives in Persia must obey their husbands. The King immediately launched a search for a new Queen and ordered that all the beautiful young women of Persia be brought to the palace for him to see and pick his new mate.

CHAPTER 2: QUEEN ESTHER

At that time, there was a Jewish man in the Persian capital, the city of Shushan, whose name was Mordechai of the tribe of Benjamin who had heard about the search for a new Queen. Mordechai had adopted his orphaned niece, Esther, as his daughter. He sent her to the palace to be a contestant but told her not to tell anyone she was Jewish and that she had a Hebrew name, Hadassah.

When Esther arrived at the palace, everyone instantly saw that she was the most beautiful woman in the land. As soon as the King saw Esther, he, too, immediately fell in love with her and made her Queen of Persia and gave her a Royal Suite and many servants. Esther remembered not to let anyone know she was a Jew.

While all this was going on, Mordechai was waiting outside of the gate of the palace where he overheard two guards plotting to kill the King. Mordechai immediately told Esther about the plan and Esther told the Captain of the Guard. The men were arrested and severely punished. The trial was recorded in *The Chronicles of the Kingdom* where Mordechai was given credit for saving the King. However, the King was not told about the plot or Mordechai's good deed.

CHAPTER 3: HAMAN

Meanwhile, inside the palace, royal life returned to normal. At a special meeting, the King promoted **Haman** to be his number one advisor and gave him a special, royal ring. Now **Haman** was an evil and very vain man. He ordered everyone in the palace (except the King) as well as everyone on the street to bow before him.

One day, **Haman** went outside the palace. All the people knelt before him except for Mordechai because Mordechai was a Jew and Jews only kneel before God. **Haman** was furious. He ordered that Mordechai and all the Jews be arrested and executed. To pick a date to annihilate the Jews, **Haman** created a lottery in which a *pur* or a "lot" would be chosen randomly. The "lots" or *Purim* were made and **Haman** picked the lot for the thirteenth day of the month of Adar to destroy the Jews of Persia and seize their property. **Haman** then sent an order to his secret police to make their plans and annihilate the Jews on the thirteenth of Adar.

CHAPTER 4: AT THE PALACE

Mordechai learned of **Haman's** evil plan and immediately warned the Jews who became very afraid.   Meanwhile, back in the palace, Esther also learned about the order to murder the Jews and requested that Mordechai secretly meet with her and discuss the situation.

Mordechai told Esther what was happening and he asked her to be strong and find a way to save herself and her people. Esther explained that the law of the land prohibited her from speaking to the King without his permission or she would be punished and lose her crown. Mordechai asked her to find a way to get word of **Haman's** plan to the King.

Esther promised to make a plan and tell the King before the thirteenth of Adar.

CHAPTER 5: THE INVITATION

Three days later, Esther put on her most beautiful clothes and went to the royal garden where the King liked to walk. When he saw her, Ahasuerus was overwhelmed by her beauty. He held out his golden scepter and gave her permission to speak. He promised her he would give her anything, even half of his kingdom.

Esther had a plan. She asked the King to join her for a special feast and requested that he should only bring **Haman** with him to the repast. The King immediately sent word to **Haman** who, being vain, was glad to be invited not knowing that Esther had set a trap for him.

Pleased by the invitation, **Haman** left the palace so that all the people in the street would bow down to him. Yet again, Mordechai refused to bow down to **Haman.** Infuriated, **Haman** hurried home in a rage. He told his wife, Zeresh, about Mordechai and the Jews. She said, "HANG THEM ON THE GALLOWS" and so gallows were built in every province of the Kingdom of Persia.

CHAPTER 6: HONORING MORDECHAI

That night, the King could not sleep and ordered his servants to read to him from *The Chronicles of the Kingdom*. That is how the King learned Mordechai had saved his life. The King then sent for **Haman** and ordered him to make a special parade for the King's favorite person. **Haman,** being vain, assumed he was the person to be honored, so he ordered a grand parade to be held in Shushan.

Haman asked the King, "Who is the man the King wishes to honor?" **Haman** was shocked when he learned that it was Mordechai who was to be honored. Trembling, Haman left the palace and again ran to tell his wife, Zeresh, the bad news.

Zeresh warned **Haman** that Mordechai and the Jews would prevail over him. As they finished speaking, the King's guards came to escort **Haman** to the private feast Esther had prepared.

CHAPTER 7: HAMAN CAUGHT

On the second day of Esther's feast after the King had too much to drink, Ahasuerus raised his golden scepter and asked Esther what he could do for her, even up to half of his kingdom.   Esther replied that her life was in danger and pleaded for her life.

The King went crazy and asked who was responsible for this threat. Esther pointed her finger and called out, "THAT MAN, OVER THERE, IS RESPONSIBLE! THE EVIL **HAMAN**! AND HE ALSO PLANS TO KILL ALL OF MY PEOPLE, THE JEWS OF YOUR KINGDOM!" The King was furious and stormed out of the banquet hall in a rage.

Terrified, **Haman** collapsed on a banquet sofa belonging to the Queen. Before he could beg the Queen for mercy, the King returned and saw **Haman** on her sofa. Now, the King was doubly angry and ordered **Haman** and his accomplices to be sent to the gallows which he had built for the Jews.

CHAPTER 8: THE ARREST

The King's guards arrested **Haman** and locked him in the jail in Shushan. They took the royal ring and gave it to Mordechai as the King directed.

The Jews were now safe and instead of losing their lives and their possessions, were given all the things belonging to the house of **Haman**.

Haman and his henchmen were then sent to the gallows built to annihilate the Jews.

CHAPTER 9: PURIM

On the thirteenth day of Adar, **Haman** and his followers were punished by royal decree.

The next day, on the fourteenth of Adar, a Jewish festival was proclaimed. It was called Purim. Purim was declared to be a very special day on which *"sadness became happiness and mourning became joy"* for the Jewish people. From then on, all the Jews in the world have celebrated Purim every year on the fourteenth of Adar. On Purim, Jews give MISHLOACH MANOT (gifts) to one another and TZEDAKAH (charity) to the poor to remember the heroism of Esther and Mordechai.

And, so, the Jewish people established Purim as their happiest holiday and continue to celebrate it to this day with carnivals, special songs, Purim plays, the wearing of masks and, of course, booing the name of **Haman!**

The end.

HAPPY PURIM!

GLOSSARY

- **Adar:** Twelfth month in ancient Hebrew calendar and the sixth month in the current Jewish calendar. On leap years, there are two months of Adar. Purim is celebrated during Adar II.
- **Ahasuerus:** King of Persia, perhaps derived from Xeres.
- **Esther:** Of ancient Middle Eastern origin, perhaps meaning "star." Second queen of Ahasuerus and heroine of the Purim Story.
- **Ethiopia:** Most distant southwest province of the Persian Empire, located in Africa.
- **Hadassah:** Hebrew name of Esther meaning "myrtle," a symbol of hope.
- **Haman:** Evil Vizier of Persian Empire, descendant of Amalek, ancient enemy of the Jews.
- **India:** Most distant eastern province of the Persian Empire
- *Megillah:* Scroll (Hebrew)
- *Megillat Esther:* Scroll of Esther (Hebrew)
- *Mishloach Manot:* "Sending of portions," (Hebrew) special Purim gifts including three cornered pastry called *Hamantaschen* (Yiddish) or *Ozenai Haman* (Hebrew). Also called *Shalach Manos* in Yiddish.
- **Mordechai:** Uncle and adoptive father of Esther, descendant of tribe of Benjamin
- *Pur:* A "lot" or a small stone used in a lottery or raffle
- **Purim:** Literally "lots," also name of the holiday of Lots celebrated on the fourteenth of Adar
- **Shushan:** Capital city of Persian Empire, perhaps modern city of Susa, Iran
- *Tzedakah:* Charity or alms (Hebrew)
- **Vashti:** First (and deposed) wife of Ahasuerus
- **Zeresh:** Wife of Haman

CONTRIBUTORS

Lance J. Sussman, Ph.D. was appointed Senior Rabbi of Reform Congregation Keneseth Israel (KI) in Elkins Park, PA in 2001. A historian of the American Jewish experience, Rabbi Sussman is a prolific author and popular public speaker. He also served as Chair of the Board of Governors of Gratz College and has taught Jewish history at Princeton, SUNY Binghamton and Hunter College. Sussman lives in Center City Philadelphia.

Marlene D'Orazio Adler is a multifaceted, widely exhibited artist and art educator. Her media are papermaking, printmaking and photography. She is inspired by nature and spirituality and often uses symbols to convey her ideas. She is Chair of the KI Temple Judea Museum Artists Collaborative. Various genres of her work are permanently displayed at KI where she regularly exhibits in the synagogue's Temple Judea Museum. Adler is a native Philadelphian who lives in Glenside, PA.

CPSIA information can be obtained
at www.ICGtesting.com
Printed in the USA
BVHW021916250222
630107BV00001B/1